News Travels *Fast*

Printed in Mexico

ISBN-13: 978-0-15-352729-6
ISBN-10: 0-15-352729-3

1 2 3 4 5 6 7 8 9 10   050   11 10 09 08 07 06

Harcourt

SCHOOL PUBLISHERS

Visit *The Learning Site!* www.harcourtschool.com

In the Past

Sharing news and ideas is called communication. In the past, people drew pictures on rocks to share news. Later, people wrote books by hand.

▼ Cave painting

The printing press made it easy to make books and newspapers. People could learn the news quickly.

▼ Early printing press

Big Changes

Other things changed communication, too. Telephones let people talk at any time. Radios and TVs bring news into our homes.

Computers make communication easy. The Internet helps people everywhere communicate. You can send mail to a friend without paper.

In the Future

Communication keeps getting faster. Once it took weeks to learn the news. Today, people get the news when it happens.

How will people communicate in the future? Your watch may be a telephone. You could talk on the phone by using your watch!

E-Paper

A new kind of paper is called electronic paper, or e-paper. It is light and thin. It can be used over and over. One day soon, newspapers may be printed on it.

Think and Respond

1. How did people share news long ago?

2. Name one invention that changed how people communicate.

3. Why is it helpful to get the news as it happens?

4. How do you think communication will change?

 ## Activity

Work with a partner. Act out one way people share news and ideas.